# Nottingham

CW00430655

*on old picture po*

## David Ottewell

1. One of the earliest picture postcards of Nottingham Castle, published at the time when the message had to be written on the same side of the card as the picture. Published by Boots, it was posted back to Nottingham from Burton-on-Trent on 29 August 1901.

**Designed and published by Reflections of a Bygone Age, Keyworth, Nottingham 2005**

**Printed by Phase, Underwood, Nottinghamshire**

£3.95

# Introduction

Nottingham Castle is nationally, and indeed internationally, known because of its association with the legend of Robin Hood. Sadly for those visiting the castle today, the building probably fails to live up to the image they have. William the Conqueror ordered William Peveril to build the first castle in 1086. This was of the motte and bailey type with wooden buildings. By the reign of Henry I (1100-1135), the first stone walls had been built.

Two monarchs, Henry II and Henry III, were responsible for raising the status of the castle. The former built walls of stone and added several new buildings. The latter, who was King for 56 years, spent a lot of time at the castle so the apartments were lavishly fitted out and accommodation built for his entourage and servants. He also added to the castle defences. From this time until Richard III rode from Nottingham to his death at the Battle of Bosworth in 1485 Nottingham castle was undoubtedly at its height.

During Tudor times and until the Civil War, the castle went into decline and was little used. During the Civil War, Parliamentary troops held the castle under Colonel Hutchinson and repulsed Royalist forces. Following the conflict it was decided to knock down what was left of the castle.

The Duke of Newcastle bought the castle site, removed much of the castle remains and by 1679 had built a large house. For the next century it was one of the family's main residences. From the 1770s it became a lower priority to the family and was used first as a boarding school and then apartments.

In October 1831, the unoccupied ducal mansion was looted and fired by a mob supporting the Reform Bill. After standing derelict for 50 years, the building underwent restoration and in July 1878 opened as a museum. Thus visitors today are greeted by the sight of the restored seventeenth century ducal palace rather than a medieval castle.

Picture postcards, first published in Britain in 1894, became popular in 1902 when legislation allowed a message to be written with the address on one side of the card, with the other side reserved for the picture. From then until the First World War, millions of postcards were posted daily: a quick, reliable means of communication in an age of few telephones. As a popular tourist attraction, many postcards were produced featuring aspects of Nottingham Castle by both local and national publishers. It is from this wealth of material that the illustrations in this book were selected.

David Ottewell
December 2005

*Front cover:* A Charles Flower painting of a view from within the Park area. Thomas Chambers Hine was mainly responsible for laying out the Park Estate using a geometric design. Many of the older houses in the estate were designed by him or his partners. Postcard published by the famous and prolific national firm of Raphael Tuck as *Oilette* series 1783.

*Back cover (top):* The double flight of steps, totalling 38, provided access to the eastern entrance of the Ducal Mansion. The front door, on the first floor, was reached by a further set of steps. The Robin Hood Rifles used the eastern terrace as the venue for their drill practice. *Clumber* series postcard no. 97, published by Albert Hindley of Clumber Street, Nottingham.

*Back cover (bottom):* The bandstand dates from the latter part of Queen Victoria's reign when Nottingham Corporation took a 500-year lease on the castle and grounds and began a programme of re-development. *Clumber* series no. 44.

NOTTINGHAM CASTLE FROM THE AIR.

**2.** An aerial view of the Castle from the west, showing the Ducal Mansion to be a horseshoe shape. To the left is the Castle Green, beyond which can be seen the nurses' home and General Hospital complex. Behind the Castle, on the eastern side, paths radiate from the Victorian bandstand.

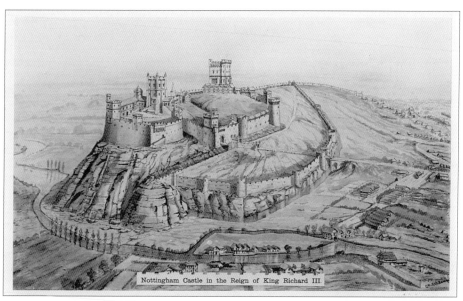

Nottingham Castle in the Reign of King Richard III.

**3.** The Castle Rock was a naturally defensive place on which to build a castle. The first castle, of motte and bailey design, was built in 1086. Gradually stone replaced the original wooden buildings. This artist's impression of the castle in the reign of Richard III shows it extended over a large area.

**4.** Mortimer's Hole. Roger Mortimer, Earl of March, was the lover of Edward II's wife, Queen Isabella. After the death of her husband the pair usurped power. Many objected, not least Isabella's young son, the rightful monarch, Edward III. In November 1330, supporters of Edward III entered the castle via a passageway running from the base of the western wall. Mortimer was captured, taken to London and executed at Tyburn. *Rex* series postcard.

**5.** At the end of the fifteenth century, Nottingham Castle was at the height of its glory with extensive accommodation. However, during Tudor times it was allowed to fall into disrepair. Another artist-drawn postcard published by locally based company C and A G Lewis, postally used in October 1920.

NOTTINGHAM CASTLE IN THE 17th CENTURY
CHARLES I RAISING HIS STANDARD AUGUST 25, 1642 BY HENRY DAWSON.

CITY OF NOTTINGHAM
ART MUSEUM.

**6.** A copy of a painting by Henry Dawson, held in the Castle collection, showing Charles I raising his standard on Derry Mount to signal the start of the Civil War between the Royalists and Parliamentarians.

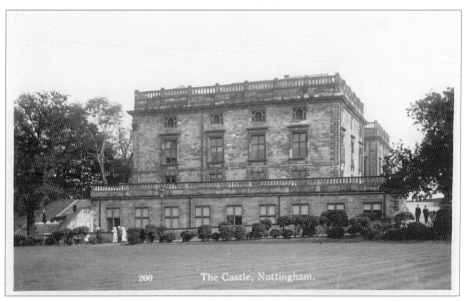

200          The Castle, Nottingham.

**7.** In 1674, the First Duke of Newcastle bought what was left of the castle. He had much of the site cleared and a modern mansion built. Work was completed in 1679 and for the next century this was one of the family's principal homes. This postcard view published by C and AG Lewis shows the mansion from Castle Green.

Nottingham Castle

**8.** A rural scene close to the western edge of the castle. Originally the area from Castle Rock to the River Trent was meadow land, famous for its wild flowers, especially crocus. It wasn't until the nineteenth century that most of this land became filled with housing. The area became known as The Meadows, reflecting its origins. Valentine of Dundee published this postcard.

The Castle Entrance, Nottingham.

**9.** The Castle gateway was built during the reign of Henry III, at the same time as the outer bailey walls. By 1904, when this postcard was posted, it was looking a little the worse for wear. *Woodbury* series card published by Eyre & Spottiswoode of London.

**10.** Between 1908 and 1909, extensive renovation work was carried out on the outer bailey walls, and Farmer and Bradley of London were employed to work on the gateway, which retained its basic shape except for the demolition of the lodge to the right hand side *(see illustration 9)*. C and AG Lewis postcard.

CASTLE GATEWAY, NOTTINGHAM

**11.** The building to the left of the castle gateway was the riding school built for the Nottingham troop of the Yeomanry Cavalry in 1798.

ANCIENT GATEWAY. NOTTINGHAM CASTLE

ROBIN HOOD STATUE. NOTTINGHAM

**12.** By the First World War, the Riding School was in a dilapidated state and it was finally demolished in 1926. The resulting gap exposed two fourteenth century archways that spanned the outer moat, allowing access to the castle grounds.

**13.** The space formerly occupied by the Riding School was used to celebrate Nottingham Castle's association with Robin Hood. A statue of the notorious outlaw, designed by James Woodford RA and paid for by local businessman Mr Philip Clay, was unveiled by the Duchess of Portland in July 1952. In addition to Robin Hood's statue, two others were erected featuring members of the band of outlaws. A set of four reliefs, illustrating well-known tales from the Greenwood, was also fixed to the castle walls. The card was posted to Grimsby in 1957.

**14.** A constable stands proudly on duty by the castle gateway prior to its renovation in 1908. There was always a permanent police presence at the castle during this period. After passing through the gateway, people had access to the lower bailey: alternatively they could go straight forward through the metal gates.

**15.** A postcard published prior to the First World War by Charles Voisey of London shows the intricate ironwork that had gone into the construction of the castle gates and the gas lamp standards that surmounted them.

NOTTINGHAM — The Castle Gates

**16.** The entrance to the main castle grounds seen from the inside. The two pointed wooden huts were known affectionately as 'pepperboxes'. Postcard published by C and AG Lewis.

**17.** Further alterations to the castle entrance took place in 1927, including a new carriage access, seen to the left. The road beyond it is Friar Lane, leading to the centre of Nottingham. On the skyline is the dome of the Council House, opened in 1929 to replace the old Exchange. *Rex* series postcard from the early 1930s.

THE CASTLE, NOTTINGHAM.

**18.** Once inside the grounds the visitor had a choice of paths in order to reach the Ducal Mansion. Each route was flanked by lawns and flower beds. Card published by WH Smith, and posted to Manchester in 1913.

CASTLE RAVINE, NOTTINGHAM.

**19.** Posted at Arnold in April 1906, this *Clumber* series card (no. 105) reveals a typical scene in the castle ravine. In fine weather, parents or the family nanny would bring children up to the castle to enjoy the open spaces.

**20.** An idyllic scene within the grounds, published as a postcard by the well-known publishing firm, Bamforth of Holmfirth, more famous for their comic and song cards.

**21.** This pathway led to the western side of the castle. Originally, as on the eastern side, entry to the Ducal mansion was gained at first floor level. WH Smith *Kingsway* series postcard.

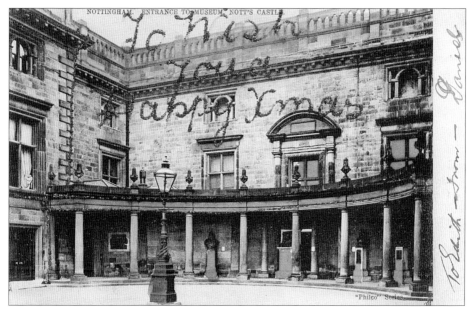

**22.** Before famous local architect TC Hine remodelled the castle in the 1880s, the central window - seen here with the arched top - was the entry point to the castle leading into the main hall. The ground floor contained the servants' hall and other minor rooms. This postcard, by the Philco Publishing Co, was posted to Wymondham on Christmas Eve 1904. The colonnade features busts of five locally-born or based writers: Philip James Bailey, William and Mary Howitt, Lord Byron and Henry Kirke White.

**23.** An early twentieth century view taken from inside the grounds. This was posted to Leeds on 23 December 1902, with Christmas and New Year greetings appended.

7TH BATTN. (ROBIN HOOD) SHERWOOD FORESTERS.
( NOTTS & DERBYSHIRE REGIMENT.)

**24.** The Robin Hoods, 7th Battalion of the Sherwood Foresters, were based in the old Riding School next to the castle walls.

**25.** A war memorial to the Sherwood Foresters in the castle grounds. The famous Nottinghamshire regiment was awarded 14 Victoria Crosses during the Indian Mutiny, Boer War and First World War.

WAR MEMORIAL
17th (Notts. & Derbys.) BN. SHERWOOD FORESTERS
NOTTM. CASTLE GROUNDS

(COPYRIGHT, WHITBY AND COLLINS).

NOTTM. CASTLE MUSEUM GROUNDS, JUNE 21ST, 1906.

**26.** The bemedalled members of the Nottingham and Notts Crimean and Indian Mutiny Veterans' Association pose for the camera in the castle grounds during their reunion on 21 June 1906. It is interesting to note two females amongst the group. Posted to Newark in August 1906, the card carried the message: *"I am enjoying myself very much, but not for long for school begins next week"*.

Captain Albert Ball V.C Memorial
Castle Grounds

**27.** The memorial to Albert Ball VC, the most famous Nottingham-born combatant of the First World War. As a member of the Royal Flying Corps, he shot down 43 enemy planes and a balloon before being killed himself, aged only 20.

**28.** The 21-foot tall bronze memorial to World War One flying ace and local hero Albert Ball, crafted by sculptor Henry Poole, shows him in flying gear with a female figure, symbolising 'air', standing behind him. The statue was unveiled by Air Marshall Trenchard on 8 September 1921. Postcard published by SC Cresswell of Nottingham.

**29.** *Rex* series postcard from the 1920s, with a view of the Nurses' Home behind the Albert Ball Memorial.

NOTTINGHAM CASTLE.

**30.** Tom Browne, one of the most famous postcard illustrators of the Edwardian era, was born in Nottingham in 1870. His colourful life saw him running away from school, aged 11, to take up an apprenticeship with a firm of lithographers. A gifted watercolour artist, most of his postcard designs were on comic themes. This picture of Nottingham Castle, published by Davidson Bros, is one of his few topographical views.

NEW GATEWAY, NOTTINGHAM CASTLE.

**31.** An unorganised assortment of smartly-dressed children outside the main Castle entrance is featured on Albert Hindley's *Clumber* series postcard no. 47. *"Will you please send someone to the Midland station to meet me Thursday about 5.45"*, wrote the sender of the card, posted to Leicester in September 1919.

CASTLE GATEWAY & DRILL HALL, NOTTINGHAM.

**32.** The Bulwell stone-fronted tower was added to the Riding School in 1871 when the Robin Hood Rifle Corps took over the building. *Clumber* series postcard no. 133.

Castle Gates, Nottingham.

**33.** Another *Clumber* card, no. 373, featuring the metal gates, which formed the entrance to the grounds of the museum itself. A turnstile regulated entry.

Entrance to the Castle Grounds, Nottingham.

**34.** The skyline on this c.1905 postcard view is unrecognisable today, and the tree-studded entrance has the look of a park rather than a city castle.

CASTLE GROUNDS & MONUMENT, NOTTINGHAM.

**35.** Unveiled on 3 July 1884, the obelisk, situated just inside in the castle grounds, is a memorial to local men who lost their lives in the Afghan Wars of 1878-80. The 59th Regiment of Foot, raised locally, lost 42 men in Afghanistan. *Clumber* series card no. 384.

KING CHARLES **THE CASTLE GATE** KING EDWARD III Proceed
HOISTING THE STANDARD **NOTTINGHAM.** To The arrest of MORTIME

KING CHARLES I

MORTIMER'S HOLE

R.P.Phillimore

**36.** The postcard artist and publisher Reginald Phillimore was born in Nottingham in 1855. His father was the doctor at the local Asylum. Later, Reginald moved to North Berwick, from where he produced over 700 postcard designs, including this one of his home town. All were paintings by Phillimore himself, and featured mostly historical scenes.

**37.** A view of the Castle bandstand published in the late 1920s by Spree, a prolific Nottinghamshire photographer. The card was posted from Arnold to Skegness in August 1922.

**38.** Over the years, many entertainments have taken place on the Castle Green, once the site of the Middle Bailey. Here the Henson and Co photographer has captured a group of boys in sailor suits and girls in their bonnets performing for a well-dressed crowd.

**39.** Another *Cobden* series card published by Henson, showing a close-up view of the action at what was probably the same event.

THE HOUSE IN CASTLE ROCK.
NOTTINGHAM.

**40.** The base of Castle Rock is honeycombed with caves, some used as dwellings, but the majority for storage. The early name for Nottingham was *Tigguocobauc* (the house of caves). The Normans created fishponds below Castle Rock to provide a source of food and they stored their equipment in some of the caves. A *Peveril* series postcard, posted to Nuneaton in June 1906.

**41.** Below Castle Rock is Brewhouse Yard. As the name implies, this is the area where brewing took place to supply the needs of the Castle. It also housed two hostelries almost side by side, *The Trip to Jerusalem* and *The Gate Hangs Well*. Card published by J Valentine and Son, sent to Leicester in August 1906.

**42.** *The Gate Hangs Well* took its name from the gate denoting the entrance to Brewhouse Yard. The sign read: *"This gate hangs well and hinders none, refresh and pay and travel on"*. At the time of its closure in 1909, the licensee was Nathan S Woodward. Another Valentine of Dundee-published card.

**43.** Claims that *The Trip to Jerusalem* dates from 1189 and that soldiers departed from here to fight in the Crusades have recently been refuted. Documentary evidence shows an inn on the site from at least the sixteenth century. *Rex* series postcard from c.1930.

**44.** *The Trip to Jerusalem* is built backing onto the Castle Rock, and several of the rooms at the rear are cut out of solid rock. Some are used as storerooms for beer and wine.

MORTIMER'S ROOM.

TRIP TO JERUSALEM INN.

**45.** Mortimer's Room appears to contain a number of relics forming a mini-museum. Landlords of *The Trip to Jerusalem* have tried to exploit its historical connections to attract as many customers as possible.

Ye Olde Trip to Jerusalem Inn, Nottingham, 1189 A.D.

**46.** A 1920s view of Brewhouse Yard with *The Trip to Jerusalem* standing alone after the demolition of *The Gate Hangs Well*. The message on the postcard, sent to Birmingham in August 1930, referred to the *Trip*'s rock features.

**47.** The row of seventeenth century houses beyond the inn was built by the Duke of Newcastle to house some of his servants. In 1977 they were converted into an interesting museum - well worth a visit. Valentine of Dundee published this card in the 1960s.

**48.** The eminently suitable clifftop location of Nottingham Castle is shown in this stark view on a *Rex* series postcard, sent to Seagrave in August 1934.

**49.** This area at the base of the Castle Rock was known as *The Duke's Wharves.* It was here that the Nottingham Canal ran until it was filled in so that Castle Boulevard could be constructed. Postcard sent from Nottingham to Nailsworth, Gloucestershire, in 1912. *Clumber* series card no. 515.

**50.** A group of boys eagerly fishing on a section of the canal that runs up towards the Castle. WH Smith postcard in their own *Clumber* series, not to be confused with Hindley's.

*Nottingham is "noted" for its: Castle on the Rocks".*

*E. Hamel & Cº. are" renowned" for their "First Class Blocks".*

**51.** Hamel & Co. were famous Nottingham printers in the early twentieth century, and published many postcards of events that took place in the city. The firm also published a series of calendar postcards advertising their services. This postcard view of the Castle fulfils the same function. The example shown here was posted to a company in Bradford in June 1903.

RELIABLE SERIES 706/6

NOTTINGHAM CASTLE FROM LENTON BOULEVARD.

**52.** Lenton Boulevard, later Castle Boulevard, follows the line of the River Leen and was built in 1884. The river, a tributary of the Trent, had been diverted by the Normans to provide additional defence for the castle. Card in William Ritchie's *Reliable* series, postally used in 1908.

Nottingham Castle from Boulevard

**53.** Castle Boulevard from the opposite direction to the previous card. Trams were introduced to Nottingham in 1901, superceded by trolleybuses in 1936, and re-introduced into the city in 2004, though not (yet) along Castle Boulevard. Postcard published by Valentine.

Castle from Boulevard, Nottingham. Rex Series, No. 218

**54.** Some land at the base of the Castle Rock began to be developed in the late Victorian period, but building was spread over a number of years. The land in the foreground appears to be still in use as allotments on this postcard sent in 1925. *Rex* series postcard, sent to Ventnor in July 1925.

**55.** Judges of Hastings published this postcard showing St Nicholas's Church from the Castle. Its close proximity to the Castle meant that the church tower proved an ideal vantage point from which Royalist troops could fire on Parliamentary forces within the castle during the Civil War. As a result, the medieval church was destroyed after the attacks. A new church opened in 1682.

GENERAL VIEW FROM CASTLE GROUNDS.

**56.** A WH Smith card, sent to Sutton-on-Sea in 1912, with a view from the eastern side of the Castle. The cottages with the dormer windows were erected in 1729 as the workhouse for the parish of St Nicholas. Originally known as Workhouse Yard, they were converted to individual dwellings in 1815 when a new workhouse was built on Park Row.

Nottingham: Marshall Tallard's House.

Rex Series 335.

**57.** Built in 1675, this building became the home of Marshal Tallard who was captured at the battle of Blenheim in 1704. He was kept on parole here until 1711. It is said he discovered celery growing wild locally and was responsible for formalising its growing as a food crop in England. *Rex* series postcard.

Nottingham. The Park from Castle Grounds.    Rex Series. 308.

**58.** Originally there was a deer park attached to the castle, but by the seventeenth century it was largely unused. In the mid-nineteenth century, the Dukes of Newcastle began to develop the northern part of the former deer park. They created a private estate with some fine examples of Victorian domestic architecture, which still stand today. *Rex* series card.

PARK STEPS, NOTTINGHAM.

*Sorry I have not answered letter sooner but will write a letter later and let you know how it was...*

**59.** The Park Steps follow the course of an ancient route from Nottingham to Lenton. The steps were first cut by the Dukes of Newcastle, when they began to develop the Park area, in order to provide access from the Ropewalk down the steep cliffs into the Park Valley below. This card was published by the Scottish firm Millar & Lang in their *National* series and posted to Selston in April 1907.